Narendra Modi

www.pegasusforkids.com

© **B. Jain Publishers (P) Ltd.** All rights reserved. No part of this book may be reproduced, stored in a retrieval system or transmitted, in any form or by any means, mechanical, photocopying, recording or otherwise, without any prior written permission of the publisher.

Published by Kuldeep Jain for B. Jain Publishers (P) Ltd., D-157, Sector 63, Noida - 201307, U.P
Registered office: 1921/10, Chuna Mandi, Paharganj, New Delhi-110055

Printed in India

Contents

5   Who is Narendra Modi?

6   Birth and Early Life

11   Beginning of a Political Career

21   Becoming the Prime Minister

26   First 100 Days of Governance

29   Steps Towards a Better Nation

47   Personal Life

53   Timeline

58   Activities

60   Glossary

Who is Narendra Modi?

Narendra Modi is the present Prime Minister of the world's largest democracy, India. He is the most prominent leader of the Bharatiya Janata Party (BJP). Universally considered as a master strategist for his party, he has been the chief minister of Gujarat for four consecutive terms.

From a tea vendor to becoming the Prime Minister of the largest democracy in the world, Narendra Modi has scripted a success story that is the cause of inspiration for each one of us. What is most remarkable about his success story is that at every difficult juncture in his life, he had the courage and conviction to carve out a positive outcome for himself. He took every adverse situation head on and turned every negative into a positive. He ensured that he made all victories count, however big or small. Dynamic, dedicated and determined, Narendra Modi reflects the aspirations and hopes of over a billion Indians.

He is the longest serving chief minister of the Indian state of Gujarat, holding the office since 2001. So popular is he with the masses there that he has been successfully re-elected three times to the office. Modi is known for his astute administrative skills and has a record for being morally upright.

Birth and Early Life

Narendra Damodardas Modi, better known as Narendra Modi, was born in the small town of Vadnagar, in northern Gujarat, India. He belonged to a family of grocers in the northern Mehsana district of the state of Gujarat. Born on September 17, 1950 to a street merchant Damodardas Mulchand Modi and Heeraben Modi, Narendra Modi saw his family face many financial struggles during his childhood days.

The third of six siblings, Modi spent his childhood years helping his father in selling tea along with his brother. Despite making a living out of modest means, Modi ensured he completed his studies from Vadnagar in Gujarat. Even during his schooling years and immediately thereafter, he made his living, selling tea along with his brother on the Mehsana Railway Station to soldiers during the Indo-Pak war. The first glimpse of Modi as a great orator was seen even in his schooling years. In the recent interviews conducted with his school teachers, they have recounted that while Modi was an average student, he always received praises for his great debating skills and had the power to sway audiences with his speeches. His school friends remember that as a child also he was very industrious, having an affinity for debates and a curiosity for reading books. They further recollect how Modi used to spend many hours reading books in the local library.

As a child, Modi always felt a strong urge to make a difference to society. He was much influenced by the life and works of Swami Vivekananda, which laid the foundation of his journey towards spiritualism and inspired him to pursue the mission to fulfill Vivekananda's dream of making India a 'vishwa guru' (world leader). Modi left home when he turned 17, in order to travel across India. He travelled for two long years across the country, exploring various cultures. When he returned home, he was a changed man with a clear aim of what he wanted to achieve in life. He went to Ahmedabad and joined Rashtriya Swayamsevak Sangh (RSS)—a socio-cultural organisation working towards the social and cultural regeneration of India.

During his college days, Modi acted as the 'pracharak' (promoter) of the Rashtriya Swayamsevak Sangh (RSS). He earned an M.A. degree in political science from the Gujarat University in Ahmedabad.

Beginning of a Political Career

It was post the Indo-Pak war in 1971 that Modi joined the RSS as a propagandist. However, he continued to work in the staff canteen at Gujarat State Road Transport Corporation. His oratory skills came to use here and it was around this time that he made a conscious decision to devote himself to politics. Recognizing his contribution in the RSS and his active participation in the anti-Emergency movement during 1977, he was given additional responsibilities. With the passage of time, he was soon made in-charge of the student wing of the Akhil

Bharatiya Vidyarthi Parishad (a student body involved in anti-corruption) in Gujarat.

The party people soon realized that Modi had immense talent and what an asset he would be to the party. Hence, the RSS moved him to the Bharatiya Janata Party (BJP) in 1985. At every step and with whatever responsibility

entrusted to him, Modi proved his dedication and soon became indispensable to the party. In 1988, he became the organizing secretary of BJP's Gujarat wing, and drove the party to victory in the 1995 state elections. He was thereafter transferred to New Delhi as the national secretary of BJP.

Modi was responsible greatly in strengthening the party's presence in the state in the following years. In 1990, he was one of the BJP members who participated in an alliance government in the state, and he helped the BJP achieve success in the 1995 state legislative assembly elections as well. This allowed the party to form the first-ever BJP-

controlled government in India in the month of March. However, the BJP's control of the state government was relatively short lived, ending in September 1996.

In 1995, Modi was selected as the secretary of the BJP's national organization in New Delhi, and three years later he was appointed its general secretary. He continued to hold that office for the next three years, but in October 2001 he replaced the incumbent Gujarat chief minister, fellow BJP member Keshubhai Patel. Patel had been held responsible for the state government's poor response in the aftermath of the massive Bhuj earthquake in Gujarat earlier that year that killed more than 20,000 people! Modi entered his first-ever electoral contest in a February 2002 by-election that won him a seat in the Gujarat state assembly.

Modi's political career thereafter remained a mixture of deep controversy and achievements. His role as chief minister during communal riots that engulfed Gujarat in 2002 was particularly questioned.

Modi's frequent political success and dedication in the betterment of Gujarat, however, made him an

indispensable leader within the BJP party's hierarchy. Under his leadership, the BJP secured a significant victory in the December 2002 legislative assembly elections, winning 127 of the 182 seats in the chamber (including a seat for Modi). Projecting a manifesto for growth and

development in Gujarat, the BJP emerged victorious again in the 2007 state assembly elections, with a total seat count of 117. The party prevailed again in the 2012 polls, garnering 115 seats. Both times Modi won his contests and returned as the chief minister of the state of Gujarat.

During his tenure as head of the Gujarat government, Modi established a formidable reputation as an able administrator. He was also given the credit for the rapid growth of the state's economy. In addition to this, his and the party's electoral performances helped advance Modi's position as not only the most influential leader within the party but also a prospective candidate for the post of the Prime Minister of India. In June 2013, Modi was chosen the leader of the BJP's campaign for the 2014 elections to the Lok Sabha.

After a dynamic campaign in which Modi portrayed himself as a realistic candidate who could turn around India's underperforming economy, he and the party emerged victorious. His party, BJP, won with a clear majority of seats in the chamber and Modi was sworn in as the Prime Minister of India on May 26, 2014.

Becoming the Prime Minister

Soon after he took over as the Prime Minister, Modi's government embarked upon several reforms. He had ushered a wave of hope amidst his country people. Some of his campaigns were aimed at improving India's transportation infrastructure and at liberalizing rules on foreign direct investment (FDI) in the country.

Modi scored two significant diplomatic achievements early in his term. In mid-September, he hosted a visit by Chinese President Xi Jinping, the first time a Chinese leader had been to India in eight years. At the end of the month, having been granted a U.S. visa, Modi made a highly successful visit to New York City, which included a meeting with U.S. President Barack Obama.

The Modi wave which swept the nation was a deliberate campaigning effort by his party and one which projected him as a man of action rather than one of mere words. Using technology and social media networking sites like never before, Modi was able to easily connect to varied sections of society. His oratorical skills, his proven track record, his 'never-say-die' attitude and his 'common man' image had voters from across caste, creed, religion and financial backgrounds come out and vote for him. Modi was able to cut across all barriers, whether religious, regional or state, and establish himself as a man who dared to dream and who worked to realize those dreams.

When asked in interviews what one quality he would attribute his success to, he repeatedly mentioned his optimism and positive attitude alongside his hard work. The conviction of the man is so strong that he became the symbol of a refreshing positive change that India was looking for, away from the corruption ridden politics of the previous governments. At a time when people were getting completely disillusioned with the workings and happenings in the country, Modi positioned himself as the face of hope and one who could steer the nation towards a glorious path.

It is probably this optimism and positive energy which endears Narendra Modi to the people of India and makes him one of the most popular Prime Ministers that the country has had so far. His is a story which proves that dreams do come true and that if you dream and work towards it, nothing is impossible!

First 100 Days of Governance

When Prime Minister Narendra Modi took charge on May 26, 2014, the people of India along with the world, looked at him with high expectations. For millions of Indians, Modi had by then become the messenger of

good times. His manifesto laid stress on bringing down inflation, renewing the Gross Domestic Product (GDP) and retrieving black money from abroad, among other initiatives. As the government completed 100 days, one thing that emerged was that Modi walked the talk. During those days, the government kept itself busy picking up

tasks from its long list and ticking them as and when they neared completion. However, not everything was achievable in 100 days' time.

Hence, his actions also met with some strong criticism. Some of his initiatives that received much acclaim include bilateral relations via SAARC, the budget, FDI policy, introduction of reform bills, cleanliness campaign drives, and the digital India initiative.

Steps Towards a Better Nation

When Prime Minister Modi came to power, there was a wave of enthusiasm across India. He is perceived as a man of vision who looks at upliftment and progress from the grassroot level. In order to bring about radical changes, Modi has introduced several reforms.

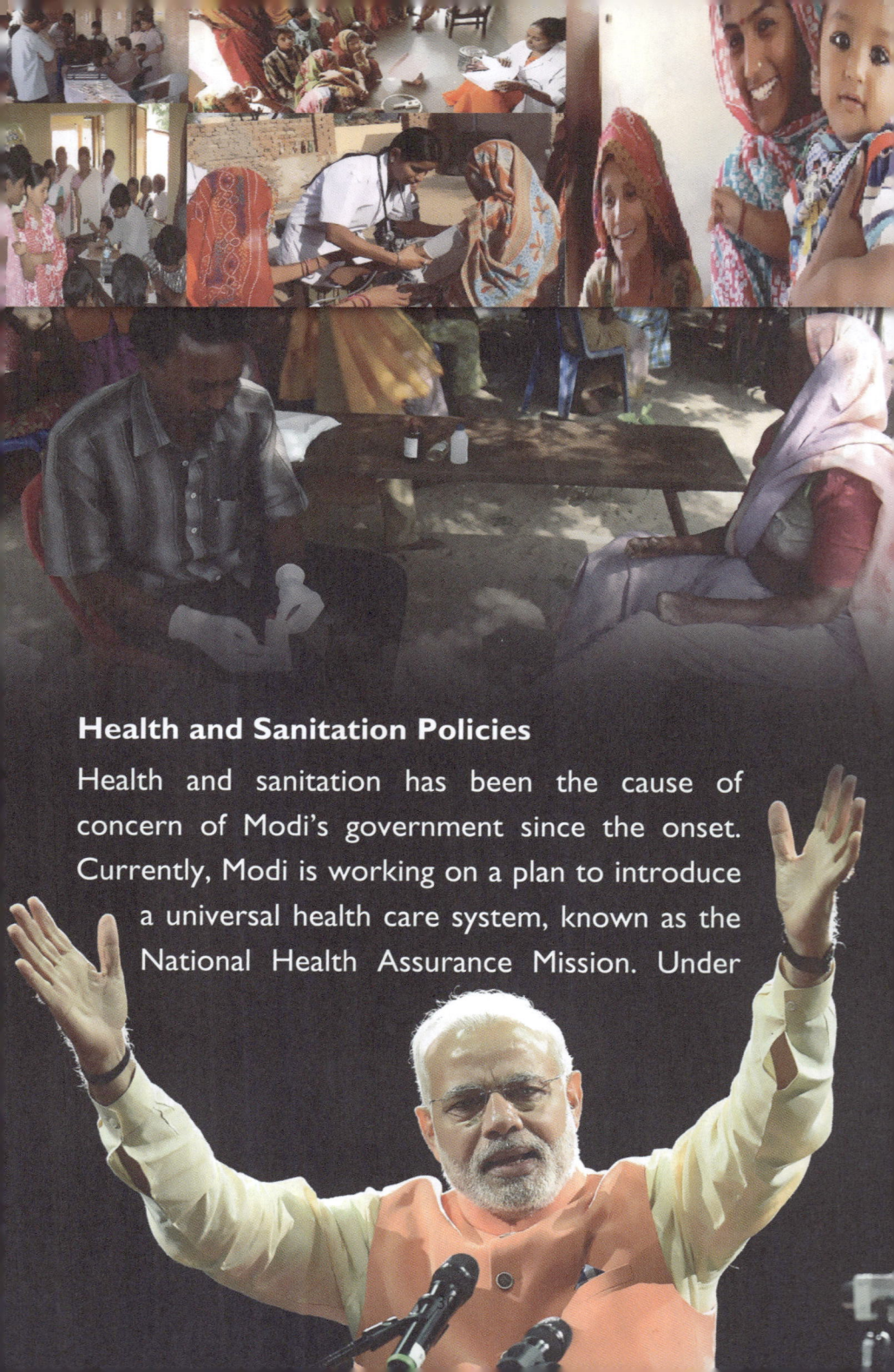

Health and Sanitation Policies

Health and sanitation has been the cause of concern of Modi's government since the onset. Currently, Modi is working on a plan to introduce a universal health care system, known as the National Health Assurance Mission. Under this plan, the government aims at providing free drugs, diagnostic treatment, and insurance coverage for serious ailments, although budgetary concerns have delayed its implementation. Another important contribution towards a better India is the 'Swachh Bharat Abhiyan' (Clean India Mission).

Swachh Bharat Abhiyan

The great leader and protagonist of ahimsa, Mahatma Gandhi had rightly said, "Sanitation is more important than independence." He said this at a time when India was under the shackles of British rule. He was aware of the pathetic situation of Indian rural people at that time and he dreamt of a clean India where he emphasized on cleanliness and

sanitation as an integral part of living. "A clean India would be the best tribute India could pay to Mahatma Gandhi on his 150 birth anniversary in 2019," Modi said as he launched the Swachh Bharat Abhiyan at Rajpath in New Delhi. On October 2, 2014, Swachh Bharat Abhiyan was launched through the length and breadth of the country as a national movement.

The mission was launched to solve the sanitation problem and waste management in India by ensuring hygiene across the country. Emphasizing on 'Clean India' in his 2014, Independence Day speech, Prime Minister Modi said that

this movement is associated with the economic activity of the country.

Modi has directly linked the Clean India Movement with the economic health of the nation. This mission, according to him, can contribute to GDP growth, provide a source of employment to thousands of unemployed Indians and reduce health costs, thereby connecting to an economic activity. Cleanliness is directly connected to the tourism and global interests of the country as a whole. It is time that India's top 50 tourist destinations displayed highest standard of hygiene and cleanliness so as to change the global perception.

Clean India can bring in more tourists, thereby increasing the country's revenue. Modi has also appealed to the people of India to devote 100 hours every year to cleanliness.

Economic Measures

From the time Modi assumed office as the Prime Minister, he worked on increasing the efficiency of India's economy and making it more business friendly. His government

worked on reforms and on streamlining the bureaucratic requirements of companies, such as the complex permit and inspection system, and numerous regulations, so as to ease the burden on companies. Modi also ordered reform among the bureaucrats of the Indian Administrative Service, who were infamous for their inefficiency and lethargic work schedule, to ensure a more efficient government.

Modi took up some important measures to help benefit the government machinery as well as the common masses. Some such measures include the following:

Mahatma Gandhi National Rural Employment Guarantee Act

The National Rural Employment Guarantee Act 2005 (NREGA) is a social security scheme that attempts to provide employment and livelihood to rural labourers in India. In an effort to make inclusive and overall development a reality, the NREGA was passed as a labour law and implemented across 200 districts of India in 2006.

By 2008, the law came to cover the entire country. The scheme was designed to provide any adult who registered for rural employment a minimum job guarantee of 100 days each financial year. This includes non-skilled work, making it one-of-its-kind across the world. It was later

renamed Mahatma Gandhi National Rural Employment Guarantee Act (MGNREGA).

The MGNREGA is an entitlement to work that every adult Indian citizen holds. In case such employment is not provided within 15 days of registration, the applicant becomes eligible for an unemployment allowance.

The Pradhan Mantri Jeevan Jyoti Bima Yojana

The Pradhan Mantri Jeevan Jyoti Bima Yojana (PMJJBY) is one of the several ambitious social security programmes initiated by Modi. It is basically a term life insurance policy that can be renewed either on a yearly basis or for a longer period of time. The policy provides life insurance coverage on the death of the policy holder.

Any Indian individual between the age group of 18 and 50 is eligible to apply for the Pradhan Mantri Jeevan Jyoti Bima Yojana. However, it is mandatory for the individual

seeking the insurance policy to have a bank account. People who avail this policy before they are 50 years old, are also allowed to enjoy the risk of life cover till the age of 55 years. However, they are required to pay the premium on a consistent basis in order to be provided that benefit.

Pradhan Mantri Jeewan Jyoti Bima Yojna

Life Insurance

Worth ₹ 2 Lacs at just

₹ 330 per annum

'Make in India' Campaign

'Make in India' is a campaign that was launched by Modi on September 25, 2014. The campaign is a highly ambitious Government of India project to attract, encourage and invite the overseas companies to manufacture their products in factories and plants located in India. This initiative, spearheaded by Modi, is aimed at generating employment opportunities for the Indian youth and accelerating economic growth by strengthening the Indian

manufacturing sector. For Modi, 'Make in India' is not just about 'FDI' in the sense of Foreign Direct Investment but it also means 'First Develop India'.

Modi announced this inventive programme called 'Make in India' in his first Independence Day speech as the Indian Prime Minister on August 15, 2014 at the Red Fort. The initiative is targeted at 25 of the most crucial sectors of the Indian economy including renewable energy, electronics, bio-technology, mining, design, manufacturing, automobiles, auto components, chemicals, railways, IT, hospitality, pharmaceuticals, tourism, aviation and textiles.

Digital India

DigiLocker is yet another Digital India initiative launched by the Modi Government in February 2015. Released by the Department of Electronics & Information Technology (DEITY), Ministry of Communications & IT, DigiLocker is an e-locker that has been designed to save one's official and other documents.

Digilocker is basically a secure personal online storage space where one can store all one's important documents. The service is open to all Indian citizens that have an Aadhaar card allocated to them. An Aadhaar card is a unique card that helps in digital identification of people for the primary purpose of tracking their social security. Each Indian citizen, when registered with DigiLocker, is allotted a storage space of 1 GB linked with his or her Aadhaar number. One can not only store their official documents like mark sheets, PAN cards, passports, certificates, voter ID cards, etc. but also store Uniform Resource Identifier (URI) link of the e-documents issued by various departments. One can digitally sign e-documents with the e-sign facility provided by this system.

There are several advantages of DigiLocker System. It empowers the citizens digitally, ensures easy availability of documents online, reduces the use of physical as well as fake documents, offers authenticity of the e-documents, and much more.

Personal Life

Narendra Modi's marriage to Jashodaben Chimanlal was arranged by the latter's parents, in keeping with the traditions of the Ghanchi caste. Years ago, when the two were engaged, Modi was 13 years of age. They got married in 1968, when Modi turned 18. The marriage took place in Modi's native village, Vadnagar, in Mehsana district.

The couple lived together for three months, after which Modi left home to travel across India, journeying as a 'sanyasi', as he described it to his family. After a period of three years, Modi stopped visiting his wife and family, as he got involved in his work as a RSS pracharak (promoter) or lobbyist. Media reports state that the marriage was never completed as Modi walked out of the marriage soon after it was solemnized.

Immediately after her marriage to Modi, Jashodaben, who had studied only till class VII, decided to complete her education. She started studying in Dholka, a city in the Ahmedabad district of the Indian state of Gujarat, and completed her school education in 1972. She then decided to enroll herself for primary teacher's course, on the completion of which she started working as a teacher.

As recollected by Jashodaben, Modi always encouraged her to study further. In an interview to a Gujarati news channel, she said that she attributed her success in life and as a teacher to Modi's encouragement.

In an interview to a leading Indian newspaper, Jashodaben spoke in detail about her relationship with Modi. When asked if she feels burdened by the

relationship, she said, "We have never been in touch and we parted on good terms as there were never any fights between us." According to Jashodaben," In three years, we may have been together for all of three months. There has been no communication from his end to this day." In

the same interview she also stated that she did not feel bad for not being acknowledged by Modi, as his wife, for all these years. She blamed their situation on destiny.

Jashodaben and Modi met for the last time in 1987, as stated by her in another interview. She also said that Modi apologized to her for not staying with her all those years and asked her to consider divorce so that she could remarry and carry on with her life. She, however, replied saying, "Why would I re-marry? You move forward on your path and I will on mine."

Though she was not physically present with her husband, Jashodaben said that she followed all his activities via media reports. In an interview she stated that she had devoured everything she could get her hands on—right from newspaper articles to watching the news. "I like to read about him," she said.

In the present time, Jashodaben lives with her older brother Ashok Modi in Unjha town of Gujarat's Mehsana district.

- **May 2014**
  - Modi was sworn in as the 15th Prime Minister of India at the Rashtrapati Bhawan, New Delhi.
  - He held bilateral talks with each visiting head of state/head of government of eight SAARC nation plus Mauritias at Hyderabad house, New Delhi.
- **June 2014**
  - Modi made his first foreign visit to Bhutan following an invitation by King Jigme Khesar Namgyel Wangchuck and Tobgay. The visit was called by the media "charm offensive" that would also seek to check Bhutan-China relations that had recently been formalized. He also developed business ties, including a hydro-electric deal, and inaugurated the India-funded Supreme Court of Bhutan building in Thimpu. While talking about the visit, Modi said that Bhutan was a "natural choice" for his first foreign destination because of the "unique and special relationship" that the two countries shared. He added that he was looking forward to nurture and further strengthen India's special relations with Bhutan. His entourage included Foreign Minister Sushma Swaraj, National Security Adviser Ajit Doval and

Foreign Secretary Sujatha Singh. He also discussed the insurgency in Northeast India and China.

- Modi went to the Satish Dhawan Space Centre, SHAR in Sriharikota, Andhra Pradesh to witness the launch of PSLV C23 carrying French satellite SPOT-7 along with other smaller foreign satellites.

■ July 2014

- In July 2014, Modi visited Brazil for his first multilateral visit.
- He met the Brazilian President, Dilma Rousseff on the sidelines of the 6th BRICS summit in Brasilia, Brazil.

■ August 2014

- The Pradhan Mantri Jan Dhan Yojana was formally launched.

■ September 2014

- Modi took a two-day trip to Japan. He met Shinzo Abe, the prime minister of Japan, at Akasaka Palace, in Tokyo, Japan.
- Modi met the Australian Prime Minister, Tony Abbott on his State visit to India and held talks on bilateral, regional and other important issues.
- PM went on a visit to Jammu and Kashmir,

where he reviewed the situation in flood-affected areas.
- Modi met Emeritus Senior Minister (ESM) of Singapore, Goh Chok Tong.
- Modi chaired a high-level meeting on Mission Swachh Bharat. He called on to Indians to make it a mass movement and link it to economic activity.
- Modi and Chinese President, Xi Jinping witnessed signing of three memorandums of understanding in Ahmedabad, Gujarat.
- Modi met Bill Gates and Melinda Gates.
- Modi unveiled the global 'Make in India' initiative.
- Modi embarked on a five-day trip to the US on an invitation by Barack Obama. He also attended the 69th session of the United Nations General Assembly in New York.
- Modi addressed the United Nations General Assembly.
- He addressed Indian community at Madison Square Garden in New York and announced sweeping changes in Person of Indian Origin (PIO) and Overseas Citizen of India (OCI) schemes.
- Modi addressed the Council on Foreign Relations in New York City.

Timeline

- **October 2014**
  - He launched the Swachh Bharat Abhiyaan and began a cleanliness drive at Valmiki Basti, New Delhi.
- **May 2015**
  - Modi launched Jan Suraksha (social security) schemes.
  - He took a trip to China.
  - He took a trip to Mongolia.
  - He took a trip to South Korea.
- **June 2015**
  - Modi took a trip to Bangladesh.
  - On behalf of former Indian Prime Minister, Atal Bihari Vajpayee, Modi received the Bangladesh Liberation War honour.
  - Modi assessed healthcare initiatives in India.
  - The first Yoga Day was celebrated, led by Prime Minister Modi in New Delhi. A gathering was held at Rajpath, a ceremonial boulevard in New Delhi, India.
- **July 2015**
  - Modi took a trip to Uzbekistan and Kazakhstan.
  - Modi embarked on a tour of Russia to attend BRICS and SCO summit in Ufa.

- He took a trip to Turkmenistan, Kyrgyzstan and Tajikistan.

■ August 2015
- Modi gave a historical speech from Lal Qila (Red Fort) on the Indian Independence Day.

Timeline

Activities

Brush Your Geography

Get an outline map of the country of India. Mark the state of Gujarat on it and colour it.

Group Activity

Form groups of five or six and make a list of three great people who have risen from extreme poverty. All these people should belong to different countries other than your own.

Make a page on each of the people you have chosen and fill information on them along with their pictures. Focus on the story of their success.

Research and Discuss

Find out from books, people or the Internet about the meaning of democracy. Form groups and discuss about it in detail in class with your teacher.

Question

1. Who is Narendra Modi?
2. When and where was he born?
3. Name his parents and mention what they did.
4. When Modi was young, what work did he do to earn his living?

5. Why do you think Modi inspires us to pursue our dreams?
6. Which quality of Modi actually helped him to actualize his dreams in the political world?
7. In which subject and which university did Modi complete his education?
8. Enumerate the political career of Modi beginning from 1977 till he became the Prime Minister?
9. Describe in brief the first 100 days of Modi.
10. What is Swachh Bharat Abhiyan?
11. What is Pradhan Mantri Jeevan Jyoti Bima Yojana?
12. Describe Modi's digital India project.

Activities

Glossary

accelerate: to increase in rate or amount

acknowledge: to recognize something as being good

alliance: a union or association formed for mutual benefit

apologize: to be sorry for something

appealed: to make a serious, urgent request

applicant: a person who makes a formal application for something

appreciation: to appreciate the good qualities of someone or something

authenticity: the quality of being genuine or authentic

budgetary: relating to or in accordance with income and spending

campaign: a course of action which is done in an organized manner

conscious: to be aware of

consecutive: following each other continuously

controversy: prolonged public disagreement

conviction: a formal declaration by the verdict of a jury or judge in a court of law that someone is guilty of something

corruption: dishonest conduct by those in power

criticism: to express disapproval

destination: denoting a place where people will make a special trip

diagnostic: concerned with the diagnosis of an illness

diplomatic: having the ability to deal with people in a tactful way

disillusioned: disappointed in someone or something

dynamic: things that change constantly

electoral: something relating to elections or electors

electronics: a branch of physics and technology

embarked: to go on board a ship or aircraft

emphasized: to give special importance or value to something

employment: the state of having paid work

empowers: to give someone the authority to do something

engulfed: to sweep over something so as to cover it completely

garnering: to gather or collect something

Glossary

glorious: someone or something that brings fame

hospitality: the friendly and generous reception and entertainment of guests

hygiene: conditions or practices favourable for maintaining health

immense: extremely large

incumbent: someone who holds a post

indispensable: absolutely necessary

infamous: someone or something that is well known for some bad deed or bad quality

infrastructure: the basic physical and organizational structures of buildings, roads and power supplies

initiatives: the power to assess and initiate things alone

inspiration: to feel the need to do something

insurance: an arrangement by which a company provides a guarantee of compensation for specified loss

juncture: a particular point in event or time

launched: to set in motion

lethargic: to be sluggish

liberalize: to remove or loosen restrictions on something

manifesto: a public declaration of policy and aims

opportunities: a set of circumstances that make it possible to do something

optimism: hopefulness and confidence

orator: a public speaker

oratorical: related to the art or practice of public speaking

oratory: public speaking skills

perception: awareness of something through the senses

pharmaceuticals: companies that manufacture medicinal drugs

pracharak: a person who spreads an idea about something

prevailed: to be widespread at a particular time

propaganda: information that is used to promote a point of view

propagandist: a person who produces or spreads propaganda

protagonist: an advocate of a particular cause or idea

Glossary

radical: drastic, major

recounted: to tell someone about something

reformations: the action or process of reforming something

registration: the process of registering

sanitation: conditions relating to public health

significant: sufficiently important

solemnize: duly perform

strategist: a person skilled in planning policies

streamlining: make a system that is more efficient and effective

technology: to apply scientific knowledge for practical purposes

transportation: to move or transport something or someone

unemployment: a state where a person does not have a job

upliftment: an act of uplifting something

vendor: a trader on the street